CALM DOWN!!

A STRESS SURVIVAL GUIDE

BY MARTIN BAXENDALE

Text and illustrations © copyright
Martin Baxendale 2007

Published by Silent But Deadly
Publications, 21 Bisley Road,
Stroud, Glos., GL5 1HF

Printed in England by
Stoate & Bishop Printers Ltd,
Shaftesbury Industrial Centre,
Cheltenham, Glos. GL51 9NH

ISBN: 978-0-9550500-5-3

FOREWORD

Martin Baxendale's amazing new theory about the existence of a Stress Monster is pure genius. His ideas will revolutionise medical thinking about the causes of stress and how to tackle them. - Prof. Klaus Klaptrapp (supplier of dodgy paid-for medical quotes and forewords to the book trade since 1933).

THANKS, PROF.

PUBLISHER'S DISCLAIMER
This book should in no way be considered a substitute for proper medical advice on stress problems, so don't blame us if it makes you worse. Should you think stress at home or at work is affecting your health, you should see a doctor.

INTRODUCTION

Martin Baxendale here, the author and illustrator of this book. You want to know what causes stress? I'll tell you. It's the STRESS MONSTER! Doctors will say that's rubbish (mine did). But it's true. I've seen him and he's out to get me...and you!

Mrs Baxendale agrees with the doctors that it's a load of bollocks. Just a symptom of my own incredibly high stress levels, excessive alcohol and caffeine intake and obsessive paranoia. But what does she know? Actually, I'm pretty sure she's in league with the Stress Monster. In fact, I suspect she's paying him to spend extra time on me. Probably hoping he'll drive me into an early grave so she can get the insurance money.

See?! There he is!! Right there, sneaking up behind me!!

5

One of the Stress Monster's favourite hiding places is in unpaid bills, overdrawn bank statements and tax demands. He waits for you to open the envelope then jumps out and scares the pooh out of you.

OH THIS IS A **BIG** ONE!! AND IT'S A **FINAL DEMAND** TOO!! GO ON, TAKE A LOOK!! THEY'RE GOING TO **REPOSSESS YOUR CA-A-R**!! FEEL THAT STRESS?!! WA-HAHAHAHAHAHAHA!!

AAAAAGH!!!

Me in sudden urgent need of a clean pair of underpants.

SPLLRRRP!

BILL

6

7

Of course, the Stress Monster's ultimate aim is to drive us all into an **early grave**...

The only answer is to avoid the Stress Monster at all costs. <u>Never</u>, <u>ever</u> open envelopes that contain bank statements, bills, tax demands, speeding fines, court summonses etc.

Leave them to pile up, file them, burn them, compost them, feed them to the dog...just <u>don't open them</u> or you'll let him out!!

13

Better still, do what I do: Get a big bottle of scotch and hide in the garden shed where there's no letter box for bills to come through, no phone, no computer, no clocks, no children, no boss...

WILL YOU COME OUT OF THERE! YOU'VE BEEN LOCKED IN THE SHED FOR **THREE DAYS** AND YOU'VE GOT A BOOK ABOUT STRESS TO FINISH!!

NO! GO AWAY! YOU'RE THE **STRESS MONSTER** IN DISGUISE!!

Garlic to ward off Stress Monsters

Stress Monster in the form of a huge hairy spider hiding in shed.

My boss, <u>Mrs</u> Baxendale.

14

Mrs Baxendale has told me I have to put some stuff in this book about the "real" causes of stress and how to fight them.

I'd better do it or she'll never stop nagging (actually I was going to put in a bit about how being nagged all the time can be very stressful, but she said I'm not allowed to)...

JUST SHUT UP AND DO WHAT I SAY!! **I'M** THE BOSS AROUND HERE!! **WA-HAHAHAHAHAHAHAH!!!**

See?!!!

(Just remember, it's really all down to the Stress Monster. It might look like there are other causes of stress but trust me, he's behind it all! He is!)

STRESS AT WORK

Problems at work, like an impossibly heavy workload, a nasty bully of a boss, and annoying co-workers, are a common cause of stress (you'll frequently find this is because your boss and annoying co-workers are actually Stress Monsters in human form).

YOU'RE DOING **UNPAID OVERTIME** ALL THIS WEEK AND I'VE GIVEN YOU A **PAY CUT! WA-HAHAHAHAHAHA!!**

...SO **I** SAID TO **HER**...BLAH, BLAH, BLAH, BLAH, BLAH, BLAH, BLAH, **BLA-HAHAHAHAHAHAHAH!!**

Constant annoying gossipy blithering (earplugs will help with this).

TAP! TAP! TAP!

How to tell if your boss and co-workers are Stress Monsters in human form. Do they say and do this kind of stuff? Yes? Then they're Stress Monsters!!

Annoying habits like noisy pencil-tapping, throat-clearing, humming, whistling, etc (here again, earplugs will help).

I've always found <u>hiding</u> is the best answer if you have a bad boss. It makes it harder for him or her to give you more work and push you around if you're difficult to find.

The staff toilet is always a good hiding place (in one job where I had a particularly horrid boss, I actually moved my desk into the toilets).

WHERE **IS** HE?!! I REALLY FANCIED HAVING A GOOD NAG AT HIM ABOUT WORKING HARDER!!

But some bosses (like <u>Mrs</u> Baxendale) are harder to fool so you may need to use more ingenuity.

My patented '**Boss-O-Hide**' office-plant disguise, available soon from all major stores. With this, you can even hide in the boss's office, where he'll <u>never</u> think to look for you!

17

On the other hand, if your boss is especially stupid, you may get away with much simpler tricks, like the good old false moustache and glasses disguise.

HAVE YOU SEEN BAXENDALE?   NO.

Ping-pong balls cut in half and painted to look like eyeballs. Stick over closed eyes while you nap for that wide-awake look.

Cotton wool plugs. Shove up nose to silence snoring noises.

Earplugs to block out annoying work noises and boring chit-chat.

zzzzz

I find taking regular naps at work is another good way to ease the stress and strain of being over-worked by an unreasonable boss. They give you much-needed breaks from your excessive work-load and also refresh you, ready for your next game of dodge-the-boss.

But it's important not to get caught, so in addition to my patented boss-avoiding disguise (see previous page) I've developed the **'Nap-O-Hide'** invention, also available soon from all major stores at a very reasonable price.

Discreet collar-hook clamps to seat-back and stops you nodding and falling forwards across desk (or clamp to optional floor-stand to keep you upright if your job involves standing up).

STRESS AT HOME

Taking plenty of naps at home is also good for your stress levels - if people will <u>let</u> you! If they won't, you may find the 'Nap-O-Hide' devices (see opposite page) for sneaky napping at work come in equally handy in the home environment...

KEEP AN EYE ON THE KIDS WHILE I'M OUT! AND KEEP WRITING OR YOU'LL NEVER FINISH THAT BLOODY BOOK!

<u>Mrs</u> Baxendale leaving for a meeting of her knitting and gin-tasting circle.

Cat about to pooh on laptop.

Me having a crafty snooze with my nap-disguise fake eyeballs.

SNORE!

WAKEY, WAKEY!!

I FEEL A WAIL COMING ON!

19

Naps can help you recover from the stress of a busy day. But they're no substitute for a <u>good</u> <u>night's</u> <u>sleep</u>. If you're feeling stressed, you should try to get at least some early nights because it can make a huge difference to how you feel and how you cope under pressure.

Unfortunately, the Stress Monster can be very persuasive...

20

Stress can cause sleep problems, in which case there are widely-available herbal remedies that can help you get a good night's sleep.

Earplugs can also help if, like me, you find night-time noise is causing sleep problems and adding to your stress levels.

SNORE!!!
WA-HAHAHAHAHA!!
SNORE!!!
WA-HAHAHAHAHA!!

WAIL!!!
WA-HAHAHAHA!!
WAIL!!!
WA-HAHAHAHA!!

Spot the Stress Monsters in human form!

Baby Baxendale - chief Stress Monster in human form!!

21

Money <u>problems</u> can be a major cause of stress, and I think I've made my views very clear on page 13 (<u>never</u> open bank statements or overdue bills 'cos you'll just let the Stress Monster out!)

<u>Mrs</u> Baxendale's advice (for what it's worth) is: "Face up to your money problems, talk them through with someone, then draw up a plan to economise and make savings".

Overdue bills, overdrawn bank statements, tax demands, etc.

Me making good use of my **'Nap-0-Hide'** secret work-place napping disguise (see page 18) to have a crafty snooze while <u>Mrs</u> Baxendale drones on and on about our money problems <u>again</u>.

Damn! Should have used the collar hook and clamp to stop my head nodding!

Children are invariably Stress Monsters in human form.

All you can do is try not to give kids anything that will make them even more stressful to be around: Like loud musical instruments, indelible felt-tip pens, sharp objects, sugar, chocolate, artificial food colourings, coffee, more brothers and sisters, etc.

I wish I'd never given ours that sodding musical tape player with a microphone and built-in karaoke mode.

I'd also strongly advise wearing earplugs at all times from the birth onwards, and especially in the first year, when you really need industrial-strength ear-defenders (but remember to take them out when you go to the pub - I forgot once and missed the landlord shouting last orders!)

23

Children can prove particularly stressful on <u>long car journeys</u>. The usual advice is to give them something to do, like a game to play, to keep them occupied.

My favourite is 'Spot The Speed Camera' with a travel sweet for the kid who's first to shout out a warning. It's saved me a fortune in speeding fines over the years.

If things get really stressful on long journeys, more drastic action may be called for.

In fact, with kids I'm all for drastic measures generally speaking, in pursuit of a less stressful life. But unfortunately <u>Mrs</u> Baxendale doesn't agree.

Holidays can be pretty stressful too. It seems most people have trouble winding-down when they go on holiday, especially if they know work is piling up while they're away. And family hols can be especially stressful.

The usual advice from <u>Mrs</u> Baxendale to me is to finish all my work before I go and "try to f***ing relax and enjoy yourself for once in your life you miserable moaning bastard!"

<u>My</u> advice would be send the family on holiday and have a nice break at home on your own. But the last time I suggested that to <u>Mrs</u> Baxendale, she thumped me and I woke up handcuffed to the steering wheel of the car with three screaming kids in the back and a map of the route to the seaside taped to the dashboard.

AND DON'T FORGET TO PACK YOUR **STRESS MONSTER**! TEE-HEE!

VERY FUNNY! AT LEAST I'M GETTING WELL AWAY FROM **HIM** FOR THE NEXT COUPLE OF WEEKS!

THAT'S WHAT **YOU** THINK! WA-HAHAHAHAHA!!!

25

COMBATTING STRESS

Apparently people under stress often start boozing more heavily, drinking more coffee, smoking more and so on. And that just makes matters worse in the long run (according to <u>Mrs</u> Baxendale - the bossy kill-joy).

I suppose you <u>could</u> try cutting down a bit on stuff like booze, coffee and fags. But in my experience, the **Stress Monster** really can be <u>very</u> persuasive.

Whisky drip-feed.

THIS IS A GREAT IDEA, **S.M.**! SAVES ALL THAT GLASS-LIFTING!

TRY THESE VODKA-FILLED PENS. THEY'RE GREAT FOR SUCKING-ON THOUGHTFULY WHILE YOU'RE COMING UP WITH NEW IDEAS FOR YOUR BOOKS.

VODKA PENS

GO ON, **HAVE ANOTHER CUP!** IT'S ONLY YOUR NINETEENTH! FANCY A DROP OF BRANDY IN IT?

THERE! NOTHING LIKE A NICE CIGGIE TO CALM YOU DOWN!

Mrs Baxendale insists <u>exercise</u> is good for stress reduction. But this is the only way she can get me inside a <u>gym</u> (and I fall for it every time!)

IN YOU GO!

Handcuffs for shackling me to rowing machine.

Authentic galley slave-driver's whip.

PUB

GYM

MRS. BAX'S GYM STUFF

Mrs Baxendale also tries to make me eat "healthy" foods instead of take-aways and fry-ups, because she read that a healthy diet's supposed to reduce stress symptoms.

Apparently porridge, green vegetables, nuts, seeds, whole grains and pulses, and other yummy stuff like that are high in magnesium, which helps calm you down.

I keep telling her, a few pints and a chicken vindaloo calm me down just fine, but will she listen?

Mrs Baxendale's breakfast - bacon and eggs!!

Health experts even reckon that <u>pets</u> are good for reducing stress. Something about watching fish swimming around and stroking cats having a calming effect, that sort of thing.

Well all I can say is they've obviously never met <u>our</u> pets.

Our cat spends all its time sleeping on my favourite chair and crapping on my computer keyboard. And if you tried stroking her, she'd have your fingers off.

And our pet goldfish spends <u>its</u> time <u>mouthing</u> <u>obscenities</u> at me through the glass. <u>Mrs</u> Baxendale says it's just my imagination, but see for yourselves.

WHO'RE YOU F***ING STARING AT?!!
YOU F***ING GORMLESS GIT!! F*** OFF
AND STROKE THE F***ING CAT!!